"*Hillary and Clinton* is about exactly what you think it's about: Hillary and Bill. But it's also about Hillary and that last name, and what it means to be attached to a reputation that is not yours alone, to always have another half that keeps you from being seen as a whole."

—**JESSICA SHAW, *ENTERTAINMENT WEEKLY***

"Hnath uncovers nuances in the Clinton marriage that suggest just what Hillary has always been up against . . . In a deeply misogynist culture, people prefer their Machiavellies to be princes, not princesses, and certainly not queens."

—**GREG EVANS, *DEADLINE***

"An intriguing, fulfilling sketch of a fantasy . . . What we're watching is the world's most competently performed therapeutic roleplay. But the therapy, as Hnath has ably constructed it, isn't for the Clintons; it is for us."

—**JESSE OXFELD, *NEW YORK STAGE REVIEW***

"Simultaneously sly and slight, *Hillary and Clinton* examines the complications of marriage, both the political and personal types . . . One thing is certain: in any universe, Hillary Clinton would never see herself as a victim."

—**BRIAN SCOTT LIPTON, *CITITOUR NYC***

"Provocative and poignant, smart and funny . . . A bold theatrical speculation and uncovering of the Hillary we didn't see, at least on either of her presidential campaign trails—a woman of surprising vulnerability trying to carve out her own space from the shadow of her forever-charming husband, but wilting in the force field of his apparent charisma and being frustrated by his own interventions into her story."

—**MARK SHENTON, *NEW YORK THEATRE GUIDE***

"Where *Hillary and Clinton* really scores is in its portrayal of Bill, who emerges as deeply flawed but fascinating—now aging out of his boyish appeal and uncomfortably out of the limelight, with no crowds to snake-charm, he's searching for a new identity."

—DAVID FOX, *PHILADELPHIA MAGAZINE*

"*Hillary and Clinton* is an audacious, whip-smart, highly entertaining piece of writing."

—CHRIS JONES, *CHICAGO TRIBUNE*

"If you disagree with Hnath's ideas, that's all right. The purpose is to provoke thought and discussion. It will."

—NEAL NEWMAN, *DC THEATER ARTS*

"Just when you would swear there was absolutely nothing more that could possibly be said about Hill and Bill, along comes Lucas Hnath's surprising and even subtle play, *Hillary and Clinton*."

—HEDY WEISS, *CHICAGO SUN TIMES*

"A play by one of America's more interesting playwrights has managed to cut through all of our emotional responses and consider [Hillary's] failures without pity, sentiment, or rancor. *Hillary and Clinton* does not pander either to HRC haters or to her supporters . . . yet it is a penetrating and astute play."

—KYLE SMITH, *NATIONAL REVIEW*

HILLARY AND CLINTON

Other Books by Lucas Hnath Available from TCG

A Doll's House, Part 2

HILLARY AND CLINTON

Lucas Hnath

THEATRE COMMUNICATIONS GROUP
NEW YORK
2026

Hillary and Clinton is published by Theatre Communications Group, Inc.,
520 Eighth Avenue, 20th Floor, Suite 2000, New York, NY 10018-4156

TCG books are exclusively distributed to the book trade by Consortium Book Sales and Distribution.

Library of Congress Control Number: 2025044138 (print and ebook)
ISBN 978-1-63670-260-5 (paperback) / ISBN 978-1-63670-261-2 (ebook)
A catalog record for this book is available from the Library of Congress.

www.tcg.org
Follow us on Instagram @tcg_gram

Book design and composition by Lisa Govan
Cover design by Mark Melnick
Cover photograph: iStock / Getty Images

First Edition, April 2026

SPECIAL THANKS

*Sarah Lunnie, Adam Greenfield, Linsay Firman,
Chay Yew, Ken Rus Schmoll,
Isaac Gomez, Carrie Chapter, Brey Ann Barrett,
Edith Freni, Hal Brooks, Val Day, Sara Garonzik,
Amy Staats, Robert O'Gorman, David Ross, Rachel Botchan,
K. Todd Freeman, Liam Craig, Matt Saldivar, Cheryl Lynn Bruce,
John Apicella, Keith Kupferer, Juan Villa, Alice Gatling,
John Procaccino, Todd Cerveris, Lindsay Smiling,
Derek Zasky, Scott Rudin, Joe Mantello,
Joey Parnes, Sue Wagner, John Johnson, Ed Wasserman,
Laurie Metcalf, John Lithgow, Zak Orth, Peter Francis James.*

PREFACE

I wrote this play twice. Once in 2008 and once in 2018.

What follows this preface is the 2018 version of the play.

The two versions have the same basic structure. The story is more or less the same. But the text itself is almost completely different.

The 2008 version of the play is stranger, wilder. I remember sitting down to write it as if I were an eight-year-old child trying to write a play about the 2008 primaries. Even the characters themselves behaved a bit more like children, at times like animals. Bill would get into physical altercations with other people. Hillary, at one point, delivered a monologue about the video game *Street Fighter II*. I was enjoying the stark disjunction between my characters and the figures we knew from the news, with a willful disregard for anything resembling bio-drama.

The 2008 draft felt like a naughty experiment, something that I was content to let sit in a drawer. I had no expectation that the play would ever see the light of day. But every so often, someone would ask about the play, and I'd let them read it. I didn't realize the play was getting passed around until 2015, when Chay Yew called me and said he'd like to produce it at Victory Gardens Theater.

In the spring of 2016, *Hillary and Clinton* had two back-to-back productions, both of which I liked very much: the one that Yew directed in Chicago and another that Ken Rus Schmoll directed at Philadelphia Theatre Company.

However, I remember trying to wrap my brain around what it meant to watch a play about the 2008 primaries during the 2016 primaries, not to mention *those* particular primaries. I couldn't discern whether it was brilliant or terrible timing. Did the audience mistakenly think I was making fun of Hillary or suggesting that she had no chance of winning? It was also during this time that folks were realizing that Trump was well on his way to winning the Republican nomination. Every week it seemed as if the circumstances had changed in some unpredictable way, and the play kept toggling between relevance and irrelevance.

I had assumed that those 2016 productions would be the last, but then I received a call in 2018 that there was strong interest in taking the play to Broadway. At first, I said that I didn't want the play to have a Broadway production. I felt as though the play's experimentation with disjunction made it cute and quirky. There was no place for cute and quirky in 2018, and I worried that it seemed as if the mismatch between the real people and my rendering of them was the subject of the play. It was not.

For me, the heart of the play has always been a battle between reason and emotion. Many of my plays are about that. *Hillary and Clinton* takes that battle and applies it to the question of how and why we elect the leaders we elect.

There's a factoid that claims that, without fail, the best-selling Halloween costume predicts the outcome of the upcoming presidential election. Similarly, I've noticed that the candidate who inspires the funniest *Saturday Night Live* impersonation *almost* always wins. It's as if the candidate who is the most fascinating "character"—whose actions and flaws best capture the public's imagination—gets the vote, rather than the candidate who is best equipped for the tasks of the actual job.

This phenomenon is part of what drew me to the figures of Hillary and Bill Clinton. It seemed as if Bill was generally characterized as the more entertaining "character" while Hillary was perceived as the boring one. But then at one key turning point in the 2008 primary, Hillary spoke at a luncheon during which it *appeared* she teared up while describing how draining it is to run for office. The moment went viral. Pundits claimed that she "found her voice." But was it the content of what she was saying in that moment, was it how she said what she said, or was it both? One half of me wants to say that, regardless, this moment should not be a deciding one as to whether this person could be a good president; the other half of me understands that a moment of vulnerability is essential to feeling that you can trust a person to represent your interests. And yet, so often emotion has the power to make us ignore facts and fall prey to decisions that ultimately betray our interests.

A similar battle plays out in my head when I write plays. I am interested in ideas. I am interested in arguments. But I also know that, no matter what, the emotional content of the play will trump the intellectual, and without it, there's no story, no play—nothing to care about. And so, in telling a story, I'm constantly negotiating between the two poles. Hillary became an embodiment of my own struggle, a character who is fighting to stay in her own story, fighting to win by reason rather than pure emotion. Her resistance to deploying emotional appeals at the cost of ideas mirrors my own.

Despite saying no to a new production, I could not resist the urge to get back into the script and give it another go. The quirkiness of the 2008 draft felt like a distraction from the battle between reason and emotion. I wanted to see what would happen if I stripped everything down to the bare essentials.

This aim was supported by the fact that the bones of the play have always been Greek—the Greeks, of course, were also keenly interested in the relationship between reason and emotion—and specifically, Sophocles's *Philoctetes* was an early influence on the play's story. And so I leaned harder into exploring argument and counter-argument and counter-counter-argument.

I started over from page one and wrote the entire play a second time. I think it took me roughly two months. In addition to thinking further about the Greeks, I found a recording of James Goldman's *The Lion in Winter* and listened to that on repeat. There's an unsentimental toughness to that play that inspired me.

I was pleased with the new draft. It felt more like muscle and sinew than the former version of the play. Despite the Broadway production being ultimately billed a "comedy," I felt as though this new take on the play was less funny and a bit harsher, sadder.

The ideal approach to this play is to let it be simple and unadorned. If something's funny, so be it; that's not the point. I think about a bit of direction I often give actors: let the sound of the thinking be louder than the sound of feeling. I'm asking actors to use arguments to compel the other character to change their mind and to do or see what they want them to do or see. If a character shouts a line, the first and easiest thing the audience will glean is that someone's saying what they're saying because they're angry. But I also recognize that, no matter what, emotions will have their way. Put them at bay, and one way or another, they'll seep in. The emotions that manage to do that are the ones that have earned their place in the performance.

I'm writing this preface in October of 2025. In about three years, it will be ten years since I wrote the second version of the play and twenty years since I wrote the first. In the play's final moments, Hillary speaks of multiverses and multiple Hillarys, and that makes me think of the prospect of multiple *Hillary and Clinton*s. I've sometimes joked that every ten years I might try writing this play again. The first iteration of the play played with the tension between real people and my imagination's version of them. The second delved deeper into two warring psyches.

I can only wonder what a third iteration might yield, though as of now I highly doubt I will revisit the play. But taking a step back, it seems that *Hillary and Clinton*, for some reason that remains mysterious to me, has become a kind of reflecting pool.

—Lucas Hnath
October 2025

HILLARY
AND
CLINTON

PRODUCTION HISTORY

Hillary and Clinton had its world premiere at Victory Gardens Theater (Chay Yew, Artistic Director) in Chicago on April 1, 2016. It was directed by Chay Yew. The scenic design was by William Boles, the costume design was by Janice Pytel, the lighting design was by Keith Parham, the sound design was by Rick Sims, the dramaturg was Isaac Gomez, and the production stage manager was Jinni Pike. The cast was:

HILLARY	Cheryl Lynn Bruce
BILL	John Apicella
MARK	Keith Kupferer
THE OTHER GUY	Juan Francisco Villa

Hillary and Clinton opened on Broadway at the John Golden Theatre on April 18, 2019. The producers were Scott Rudin, Eli Bush, Bob Boyett, Tom Miller, Len Blavatnik, James L. Nederlander, The John Gore Organization, Candy Spelling, True Love Productions, and Adam Rodner. The associate producer was Jillian Robbins. It was directed by Joe Mantello. The scenic design was by Chloe Lamford, the costume design was by Rita Ryack, the lighting design was by Hugh Vanstone, the sound design was by Leon Rothenberg, the dramaturg was Sarah Lunnie, and the production stage manager was James FitzSimmons. The cast was:

HILLARY	Laurie Metcalf
BILL	John Lithgow
MARK	Zak Orth
BARACK	Peter Francis James

Hillary and Clinton was developed by the Cape Cod Theatre Project (Hal Brooks, Artistic Director).

CHARACTERS

HILLARY—a woman running for president of the United States

BILL—a man who was once president of the United States, married to Hillary

MARK—a political strategist, a pollster

BARACK—a man who is also running for president of the United States

WHEN & WHERE

Sunday, January 6, 2008, morning, New Hampshire; also very late at night and into the next A.M.

Tuesday, January 8, 2008, early evening; also late at night, also New Hampshire

SCRIPT GRAMMAR

In general, the whole play wants to move swiftly, without breath, except where the play tells you to take a breath or pause or silence.

A space between lines indicates a very brief pause or breath. Example:

BILL

I'm trying to write another book.

I have three pages.
Working on a fourth.

An ellipsis (. . .) in place of a character line represents a fuller beat. It's a moment of thinking or rethinking or sussing or a look, a sidelong glance, etc.

Enjambments are not meant to suggest a pause or break.

Dashes (—) within lines generally bring together fragments as if they are all part of one continuous sentence. They're not meant to pause the line. Rather, move through those dashes without air. Dashes at the ends of lines indicate an unfinished thought, either because a character halts herself or because another character interrupts.

Some lines end without punctuation. This is intentional and meant to indicate that there wants to be an almost seamless flow from one character's line to the next character's line.

Slashes (/) indicate the point at which the following character's line cuts in.

PERFORMANCE NOTES

It might be tempting, very tempting, to play these characters as imitations of the real deal. An actor playing Bill Clinton might be very tempted to mimic Bill's signature Southern drawl and lip bites just as an actor playing Hillary might want to emulate her cadence and laugh. *Don't do it!* Do not play for easy recognition. Don't imitate. Don't even try to cast actors who look like these people.

Instead, imagine that the audience watching this play has never heard of the Clintons or Obama and that this is an opportunity to create these characters anew. An audience watching Shakespeare's *Henry V* has no reference point for the real Hal, nor does the actor have much of a reference point for what Hal looked like or sounded like, and therefore those performers interpreting those roles must invent the sound of the characters, the look of the characters, the physical movement of the characters, and they must base their interpretations entirely on the text and its dramatic requirements.

Treat this play in the same way. Play the text and not the persona that exists outside of the text so that you might elevate these characters beyond a facile tabloid reality.

A hotel room. A bed. Chairs. At least two doors—one leading to the outside, another leading to another room. The set feels incomplete—like a rehearsal set.

An actress walks out onto the stage. The house lights remain at full.

ACTRESS

(Holds up a coin) This is a coin. And
it has a president on one side and—
I don't know what on the other.

Now if I were to take this coin and flip it, say, five times,
I might get something like
heads heads heads tails heads—right?

And I think we can all agree that if I were to flip it another five times it would be pretty unlikely that I'd get that same exact—heads heads heads tails heads . . .

but if I were to flip it a hundred times, then sure, I would
probably get that same
order of flips once,
probably even more than once—

but if I were to flip this coin an *infinite* number of times—
well then
I'd get that same sequence over and over and over and over . . .

So what people can take from that
is that if um the universe is infinite—and some people say it is—
then that means that everything that happens in it
happens many times, over and over, and
that *that* means there are an
infinite number of planet Earths—all kinds of planets Earths—
planet Earths like this one and
planet Earths that are nothing like this one,
and planet Earths that are like this one but slightly different,
and on and on and—

So, then imagine, okay, that
light-years away from here
on one of those other planet Earths
that's like this one but *slightly* different
that there's a woman
named Hillary.

And this woman, Hillary,
is trying to become president of a country called
the United States of America.

And Hillary—she has a husband named Bill.
And Bill was once himself president.

And imagine it's Sunday, and the month is January,
and the year is 2008 on this other planet Earth—

and this is supposed to be a hotel room.

And now imagine that I'm that woman named Hillary
who lives far away from here
and who is trying to become president of
the United States of—and
I've been campaigning
for close to a year now.
I haven't slept.
I'm tired.
I'm very tired.

I have a long day ahead of me.
Events and speeches.
And the state of New Hampshire will vote on Tuesday,
in something called a primary.

(Enter Mark.)

And that's Mark—he helps run the campaign.

And every time I turn on the television,
there's someone on it saying that I'm going to lose,
and I change the channel and there's another one.
And I look at the numbers
and I look at the polls
and I look at what they're saying in the papers
and everyone says that I'm going to lose,
I'm going to lose.

And I think,
I'm going to lose

MARK

well, yes, the numbers aren't good, but—

HILLARY

they're abysmal

MARK

you're still second

HILLARY

second isn't first

MARK

it's not third

HILLARY

yeah but in Iowa I was third—
you thought I'd win Iowa

MARK

I thought there was a chance that maybe you could win Iowa, but—

HILLARY

I'm worried.

MARK

You lost Iowa, and yes,
yes, you *could* lose New Hampshire,
but we have a lot of states we know you're going to win.
You're going to be fine—this isn't the first time I've done this

HILLARY

me neither

MARK

exactly

HILLARY

right.

MARK

I'd actually be more worried if we were winning too fast—
if right out of the gate—we were at the top,
because when that happens people start to
look for someone to upset the race.
As far as I'm concerned it's good for you to be the underdog

HILLARY

so me losing is a strategy?

I wanna talk about money.

MARK

In what sense—?

HILLARY

in the sense that we don't have any,
in the sense that *because* we're losing
no wants to give us—

MARK

well look: we poll well with the poor, but
the poor don't have money.
The other guy polls well with the rich, and so he gets the money.

HILLARY

We *were* polling well with the rich

MARK

and we will again

HILLARY

not if we keep losing. The rich don't like people with the loser look and I've got—

MARK

I think you can still win this state

HILLARY

I intend to win this state,
but clearly I am not winning this state.
And if I don't win, then we're out of money,
and if we're out of money—that's it.
This is over.

MARK

Pessimism is a self-fulfilling prophecy.

HILLARY

Then give me something to be optimistic about.

MARK

He's panicking.

HILLARY

Who.

MARK

Barack.

HILLARY

No he's not.

MARK

Yes, he is.

HILLARY

How do you know that.

MARK

. . .

HILLARY

How do you know that.

MARK

Well his people called me,
earlier today they called me, and you know what they did?
They made an offer.
They said
if you pull out now, as in, if you let the next two states go,
do a sort of slow fade
out of the race, followed by dropping out entirely, then when he gets the nomination, he'd make you his running mate.

HILLARY

That's the good news.

MARK

Yes.

HILLARY

That the vultures are circling.

MARK

No, think about it—
his team wouldn't be making this offer unless
they were scared of you.
This is desperate, this is a Hail Mary—
I think you should feel
encouraged by that

HILLARY

I don't.

MARK

Okay

HILLARY

I'm offended that they would think that of me—that
that's how I'm seen
as someone who would even consider that offer—

MARK

no, that's not how you're seen.

HILLARY

I'm in this to be president—

MARK

I know that.

HILLARY

. . .

MARK

. . . Hillary?

HILLARY

Yes?

MARK

Be careful.

HILLARY

Be careful of what—?

MARK

I'm getting the feeling that
you're thinking of calling your husband,
and I don't think that that's the best kind of thing to think.
Not right now.
Maybe not ever.
But definitely not right now.
He's good where he is, which is far from here.

HILLARY

You really have a thing about my husband, don't you.

MARK

A lot of people have a thing about your husband—that's the thing.

HILLARY

He's not even speaking to me since we kicked him off the campaign

MARK

okay but—

HILLARY

I'm not calling Bill.

MARK

You promise.

HILLARY

I promise.

MARK

Really?

HILLARY

Really.

MARK

. . . Okay.

Alright.

HILLARY

Thank you, Mark

MARK

. . . Okay.

Alright.

HILLARY

. . . I know you're trying hard.

MARK

I am.

HILLARY

Okay.

(Mark exits.

Hillary is alone.)

(To audience) I pick up the phone.
I dial a number.

(Bill enters, off to the side of the stage.)

Bill?

BILL

Yeah?

HILLARY

Come to New Hampshire.

BILL

Okay.

(Hillary hangs up the phone; Bill exits.)

HILLARY

(To audience) Twelve hours later, my husband arrives.
It's night.
It's late.
It's quiet.
It's very cold.

(Knock at the door.

Hillary answers the door.)

Hello Bill.

(Bill doesn't answer. Just stands in the doorway.)

Come on in.

(Bill enters. He carries a travel bag. He puts the bag on the floor and looks around.)

BILL

. . .

HILLARY

. . .

BILL

. . .

HILLARY

. . .

BILL

. . .

HILLARY

. . .

BILL

Is this where we stayed, back in '92?

HILLARY

I don't think so.

BILL

. . . Looks really familiar, the lobby,
this room,
this view, and that uh—

HILLARY

I don't think this hotel even existed in '92

BILL

pretty sure this is where we stayed.

Strange to be back here.

HILLARY

. . .

BILL

. . .

HILLARY

You don't look like you've been eating well.

BILL

Haven't been eating much.

HILLARY

You should eat.

BILL

I forget to eat.

HILLARY

That's not good.

BILL

Yeah, I know.

HILLARY

. . . You've been busy?

(Bill shrugs.)

You said you forget to eat.
Have you been getting out of the house much?

(Bill shrugs.)

What have you been up to?

Or should I not ask?

If I shouldn't ask, I won't ask—I don't
want to know what I don't want to know—

BILL

It's nothing, Hill. Nothing.

HILLARY

Okay. Alright.

BILL

. . .

HILLARY

. . .

BILL

I'm trying to write another book.

I have three pages.
Working on a fourth.

HILLARY

I was under the impression you were traveling.
You had told me—

BILL

Yeah. That too.

HILLARY

And how was that.

BILL

Was alright.

HILLARY

Where did you—

BILL

oh, all over.
Different parts of Africa,
some time in Europe, Dubai . . . Canada

HILLARY

and that was because of—

BILL

Charity work.

HILLARY

Alright. Okay. Well that's—

BILL

who knows if it's actually something that does anything that's—

HILLARY

now I'm sure it's very—on a certain level, regardless—
very satisfying

BILL

I just like being useful.

HILLARY

. . .

BILL

—had some stomach stuff,
while I was overseas, had some—
problems with my stomach,
terrible stomach pains

HILLARY

hope you got that checked out, Bill—

BILL

no, I did but it kept on like that
even after they gave me some pills, so
when I was in Croatia I went to some kind of "witchdoctor"—
is that what they're called—?

HILLARY

I doubt it.

BILL

—because I thought, well nothing else is working,
nothing else is taking away the terrible feeling in my gut,
why not give this a try—so I went to this guy,
and you know he did his thing, he did what
"witchdoctors" do, I guess, did some things
and said some words
that I didn't understand—prayers of some kind probably—
and at the end of it he looked at me straight in the eyes
and said:
"you're cursed."
He said, "You're cursed, you're a cursed man, I
can see it hanging around your neck,
this thing, this curse"—and that, something about that just really pissed me off, just really—
and I said to him, "I came to you for help with my stomach."
He said, "Yes, and I fixed that, but I also think you're cursed."
He said, "For some time, you've been cursed."
And then he asked for more money to remove the curse,
and I was so angry—I really just blew my lid—said some things I probably should not have said,
and then I stormed out.

HILLARY

. . . I do wish you would try a little harder to control the things you say

BILL

yeah well . . .

And how are you?

HILLARY

I'm good, Bill. I'm good, I'm—
I'm running for president.

BILL

You are.

I was surprised you called me.
I didn't expect that—I didn't
expect you to ask me to come out here.

HILLARY

I wanted to see you.

BILL

You didn't want to see me before.
Why do you want to see me now?

HILLARY

Some time has passed and—

BILL

You told me to go home,
that you didn't want me around

HILLARY

and at the time, I didn't want you around.

BILL

You sorta kicked me out—you know, you sorta—
and so there I was spending Christmas alone—
our kid off with her boyfriend's family
and you were off with your mother—

HILLARY

could have spent Christmas with either of us

BILL

the boyfriend's parents don't like me

HILLARY

they like you enough to put up with you for one day

BILL

and your mother is always looking at me like she's judging me
and I don't need that crap.
So I just stayed home and I made a turkey loaf and
instant mashed potatoes—
smoked a cigar, watched some TV, and played with the dog.

HILLARY

. . . well you're here now.

BILL

. . . yeah.

HILLARY

. . .

BILL

Can I touch you . . . ?

HILLARY

. . .

BILL

. . . it's been so long.

HILLARY

Alright.

(Bill walks over to Hillary and gently places his forehead against her shoulder and just holds it there.)

BILL

I missed you.

HILLARY

I missed you too, Bill.

(She strokes his head.)

BILL

I'm not very good by myself.

HILLARY

I know.

BILL

I don't like being alone.

HILLARY

I know.

BILL

I miss this.
You miss this?

HILLARY

. . . I do.

BILL

I don't see you enough.

HILLARY

I know.
I know.

BILL

Do you like being out here,
doing this—doing the—the campaigning and—?

HILLARY

I do

BILL

well that's good. It can be a real slog if you don't, a real pain in the—

HILLARY

No, I find it a relief in a way—it's very exciting,
very satisfying.

BILL

That's good.

HILLARY

It's a lot of work.

BILL

It *is* a lot of work

HILLARY

but I'd rather be busy than not.
I'm happiest when I'm busy

BILL

yep, I know what you mean

HILLARY

—not without its stressful moments

BILL

oh sure

HILLARY

so much to keep track of, everything's always changing,
there are the worries, the occasional—the frequent—
But no, it's good—it's—things are good.
Going out, talking to people,
seeing different parts of the country—
the staff, and Mark—

Mark, he's doing good work.

BILL

What are you worried about?

HILLARY

What's that?

BILL

You said you were worried.

HILLARY

I did, yes . . . Well,
since you ask:
Numbers. Money.

BILL

Money?

HILLARY

As in: We're out of money.

BILL

The entire campaign is—

HILLARY

if I don't get this state, we're not gonna make it.

BILL

. . .

HILLARY

. . .

BILL

. . . Okay.

HILLARY

So money is one of the things that I'm worried—

BILL

How much—?

HILLARY

what

BILL

money

HILLARY

do I need—?

BILL

yes

HILLARY

a lot

BILL

roughly—?

HILLARY

take the number you think I need

BILL

uh-huh

HILLARY

now triple it.

BILL

Okay.

HILLARY

Yeah.

BILL

Wow.

HILLARY

So—

BILL

That's an awful lot of money

HILLARY

mm-hm.

I'm not sure what to do . . .

BILL

. . .

HILLARY

. . .

BILL

. . .

HILLARY

. . .

BILL

Well . . .

HILLARY

. . .

BILL

Look. What can I say—it just didn't work out.
Call it a day. Come home.

HILLARY

Come home?

BILL

Come home.

HILLARY

I don't want to come home.
I'm not ready to come home.
Not yet.

Bill! Come home? Really?!

BILL

It's not working out.

HILLARY

Sure, maybe this state and the next state, but next month—
start of next month, all of those states that we have at the start
of next month—my numbers for those states
are really great.

BILL

I just don't have that kind of money.

HILLARY

Don't tell me you don't have a way of moving money around,
don't tell me that you don't get some money for
all those trips around the world—
consultation fees for your charity work—that you
can't find a way
to move from you to me.
Things will turn around

BILL

after a month of being the loser—
being the loser that everyone thought was
going to be the winner . . . ?

When you start to lose, you pull out.
Pull out fast. Don't linger. People linger.

People get up there, they lose, they die.
Then they rot. They rot in public.
Don't let them see you rot.
Don't let them see you become a
rotting corpse stinking up the place.
They see you like that, that's how they'll remember you forever.

I'm going back home

HILLARY

you're being very—

BILL

I'm offended

HILLARY

are you

BILL

you just wanted money. That's all.
That's why you called me.
You wanted me to get you money,
to use *my* ties, *my* resources, my—
to fund *your* campaign.

HILLARY

And is that such an outrageous thing to ask for?
After all the years that I stood next to you,
after all the years I waited for my chance to
step out of your spotlight—

(Bill picks up his travel bag.)

Bill, don't you walk out of here, don't you dare—

BILL

You threw me out, you got rid of me—
You said: Bill, go home.
You said: Bill, we don't need you.
You said: Bill, this is my campaign.

HILLARY

It *is* my campaign.

BILL

I know. And so I left.
I left because you asked me to.
I left because you acted like I was a turd,
like I was a disease— You acted like I was going to sabotage your campaign.

HILLARY

I didn't think you were going to "sabotage the / campaign."

BILL

Then why did you *say* that I was going to
sabotage the campaign—?
send a memo to Mark,
a memo that Mark then passed around to everyone,
a memo that said—

HILLARY

I doubt I used the word "sabotage."

BILL

I don't like being treated like shit

HILLARY

I have not treated you like—

BILL

I'm better than shit.
I'm gold. I'm golden

HILLARY

yes yes, you're . . .

BILL

people *like* me.

HILLARY

We all know people like you, but what I'm doing here is not about you

BILL

I wasn't going to make your thing about me

HILLARY

you can't help but make my thing about you

BILL

when have I ever made your thing about me?

HILLARY

Is that a real question?

BILL

Give me more credit than—

HILLARY

even when you talk about me, somehow it becomes
about you

BILL

why, because I'm good at it—? because I'm
good at talking and talking about you,
that makes it about me—?

HILLARY

eh, no, I don't think that's what I'm saying.

BILL

You are missing an opportunity here to
take the thing that I do well
and use it to your advantage.

When I ran, I won.

HILLARY

Oh—! Going there, are we—

BILL

All I mean is—what I'm / saying is—

HILLARY

If you were running today, you wouldn't win.
Especially against him.
You wouldn't have a chance

BILL

He *is* me. This Barack fellow—all the things he says out there
are the same exact things that I said when
I ran sixteen years ago,
and here everyone is acting now like it's something new,
something that no one before him has ever said, like
I've been erased, like I never existed—

I'm sorry, but do you know what it's like to have yourself taken away from yourself
and given to someone else?
It sucks.
It—

HILLARY

again we're back to you

BILL

no, all I mean is—I'm—

HILLARY

He called.

BILL

Who.

HILLARY

Him.
The new "you."
Barack called.
He called with a deal—told Mark if I dropped out now,
a gradual drop out,
he would guarantee me "running mate."

BILL

. . .

HILLARY

That got your attention . . .

BILL

. . . and you're telling me this because

HILLARY

I'm strongly considering his offer.

BILL

. . . No you aren't.

HILLARY

. . .

BILL

You're not—!

HILLARY

if I can't get the money to continue on,
what alternative do I have? No way am I
packing up and going home

BILL

caving is worse than packing up and going home.
It's a public humiliation.

HILLARY

Of you or of me?

BILL

You're senior to him—*he* should be the one begging to be your running mate,
not the other way around

HILLARY

No. I'm losing, Bill.
I'm losing really bad.
I was supposed to be number one—easy—
everyone—

every
one
expected it—number one. And right out of the gate,
not only did I not win, I didn't even come in second.

I got a bad start,
and the bad start isn't going away—New Hampshire
is just as bad as Iowa.

BILL

. . .

HILLARY

. . .

BILL

. . .

HILLARY

. . .

BILL

Alright.

Alright, I'll find a way to get you the money you need to make it for the rest of the month—

HILLARY

thank you

BILL

but . . .

I'm only giving it to you
on two
conditions.

HILLARY

. . . What condition.

BILL

Condition*s*.

Number one:
Let me join you on the trail.

HILLARY

I don't—

BILL

Hear me out.

HILLARY

. . .

BILL

Mark doesn't call the shots anymore

HILLARY

he doesn't call the shots *now*

BILL

I *know* how Mark runs things,
and you're doing things how Mark does things.

So, condition number two is that Mark is out,
and you do what I say.
I'll run things.

HILLARY

. . .

BILL

. . . so.
Do we have a deal?

HILLARY

I don't like there being conditions.

BILL

The conditions are the best part! They're worth
more than the money you're asking for.

HILLARY

You're bored

BILL

and if I am—?

HILLARY

My campaign is not a cure for your boredom.

BILL

You're chalking all your troubles up to the money,
but the money is not the problem—you're only making it about money so that you don't have to make it about the real problem, which is

HILLARY

What—Mark?

BILL

No.

You.

HILLARY

. . .

BILL

You and your opponent—in terms of ideas,
policy, platform—are basically the same—

HILLARY

no, we aren't—

BILL

basically the same.
So what it comes down to
is personality.

HILLARY

I have no interest in playing this as some likability contest.

BILL

Obviously.

HILLARY

. . .

BILL

I see what you're doing when you're out there—
I watch you at home—on the TV—and you are
so weird and wooden and stiff and—
and let's be honest, you don't even like being around people
all that much

HILLARY

of course I do—!

BILL

not people you don't know,
not the random people you have to walk up to
and shake hands with and have a little bit of
small-talk chitchat—

HILLARY

it's draining

BILL

because you hate it

HILLARY

no, because I am really listening.
Because when I talk to someone, I'm working very hard to
hear and to understand and to think about what they're saying.
I like to think they're encounters that matter more than—than—

BILL

than what I do—?

HILLARY

Just because it's harder work for me than it is for you,
that doesn't mean I'd be a bad president—
hell, I think it means I'd be a very good president.

BILL

Sure, but it also means there's no way you're gonna get elected,
and if you're not elected you're not any kind of president.

HILLARY

I refuse to believe / that people—

BILL

believe what you want—doesn't change reality.
People don't vote with their brains.

They don't—even people who think they do, don't.
It's never
not
emotional.

HILLARY

Feelings are a terrible reason for doing anything—there's too much *doing*
because of *feelings*

BILL

yeah but your problem is people don't think you have them.

HILLARY

The case I'm making for myself—

BILL

yes—?

HILLARY

the story I'm telling is that I am prepared,
that I have it together better than
anyone has *ever* had it together,
that I am experienced—

BILL

That's a shitty story.

Better to let it all hang out,
be a broken mess where you're a mess
and show the parts of yourself you're ashamed to show

HILLARY

like what, Bill

BILL

like the part of you that
when I walked in here earlier tonight
that wanted to take care of me

HILLARY

I'm not here to take care of you

BILL

make sure I was eating well,
that pet me on my head

HILLARY

I didn't pet you on the head

BILL

that's what they want

HILLARY

that's what *you* want

BILL

and I am very representative of the general public—it's why I'm so good at this.

HILLARY

I'm not interested in playing to the
lowest common denominator,
I think I'm better than that—

BILL

Yes, yes. You're better than everyone,
and you act like it all the time,
and it makes people feel like shit.
People don't like people who make them feel like shit.

HILLARY

How about if "people" grow the fuck up?

BILL

How about if you stopped being cold and stubborn
and guarded— No, I know this version of you all too well,
and if this version of you does to everyone else
what it does to me—
it's just gonna push
people away

HILLARY

oh is that right—? is that how it works—?

BILL

in my experience.

HILLARY

Your experience.
Your experience—
well maybe that is how it works in your experience,
but that is not how it works in *my* experience.
My experience with that sort of thing, I'm sorry to say,
has been very different.
My experience is that it's best to sorta kinda
keep some stuff to myself,
because when I *have* let some of that stuff out
it's not gone so well—
Didn't go so well, in fact,
when you and I were last here in New Hampshire—
back sixteen years ago—that time you seem to be so nostalgic
for—I have no idea why—I
sure as hell am not nostalgic for it—
I'm sure as hell not nostalgic for moments like

that moment when
everyone found out you'd been sleeping around,
that moment when your inability to get certain things
under control nearly cost you the entire race—
when it fell on me to go out there and tell everyone
what a good guy you were, what a good husband
you were, how you were such a trustworthy fella . . .

And *everyone* seemed to have something to say
about how I reacted—about what feelings I had or didn't have,
about how the feelings I was expressing
weren't real feelings—
It was as if the *way*
I was feeling it wasn't how other people thought I should feel—
or didn't seem to match their idea of
how a "real" person should feel, and—
And I remember I said to you—
I told you—*pleaded* with you—
please don't put me through that again.
And you promised me,
and I believed you,
but six years later you did it again.
And just before it was all gonna come out,
hit the news—I was just sitting with our daughter
in her room—she was home for Christmas
for the first time since she'd left for college, and
it was so nice to see her, because I had missed her so much.
And then you walked in and you said you had something you
needed to tell us,
and you told us what you told us.

And when you said it,
I didn't really feel much of anything,
but then I looked over at her,

and I see her crying,
and I remember I looked over at her
and I thought "isn't that strange—
I don't feel any of that."

I used to feel that.
But not anymore, because
you know you get told enough times that your feelings
aren't real—at a certain point you sorta stop
feeling what you're feeling.

And I looked at her—at our daughter—
and she had all of that—and I actually
felt kind of jealous of her—and do you remember
what I said to her—

BILL

. . .

HILLARY

I said, good girl, good girl.
you have yourself a good cry,
you hold on to that.
I said, You're crying now and maybe
you don't like how you're feeling,
but you hold on to that for as
long as you can.

And she ran out of the room and I
asked her to stay but she had already gone,
And then I just sat there, just sat there staring at a wall.

Then I remember you said you wished I would cry,
because if I cried that would mean I could still feel hurt.

And if I could still feel hurt,
then that would mean I could still feel for you.

And you asked me, “Do you feel for me?”

And I told you I didn’t know,
and you told me that you were scared—scared that
if I didn’t feel for you that I was going to divorce you.

And I told you I wouldn’t do that—I wouldn’t divorce you,
and you asked me if I was sure,
and I said, “Yes.”
I said, “I’m with you. I’m with you. ’Til the end I am with you.”

BILL

. . . And every day I am so grateful for that.

HILLARY

I’m not not a broken mess because
I’m trying to play like I’m perfect.
It’s just that those things that are supposed to make me
cry just don’t make me cry anymore.
I just don’t have it in me.

This is what I’ve been through, Bill.
I don’t cry.
I keep it together. No matter what, I keep it together.

BILL

. . .

HILLARY

. . .

BILL

. . .

HILLARY

. . . What.

What are you thinking.

BILL

No, just that—

HILLARY

say what you're thinking . . .

. . .

BILL

. . . if you were to just say all of that—out there—out in public—you'd win.

HILLARY

. . .

BILL

. . .

HILLARY

I don't need your money.
Mark and I will figure out something else. I'm not going to be your puppet.

Mark stays where he is. You stay where you are, which is
not on the trail,
not speaking for me, *not* telling me what to do.

You can go now.

BILL

It's late, Hillary.

HILLARY

Yes, and—?

BILL

I have nowhere to go.
There's nothing at home.

HILLARY

It was a mistake to call you out here.

BILL

Don't say that, don't say that, Hill . . .

HILLARY

. . .

BILL

. . .

HILLARY

. . .

BILL

Can I at least sleep here tonight?

HILLARY

I don't want that.

BILL

Just that it might raise more questions if someone sees me here and sees me not staying with you, it might—

HILLARY

alright.

BILL

. . .

And do you think it would be a problem if I stuck around tomorrow too, just while you're in New Hampshire, that's all—

HILLARY

I don't know. I don't—don't ask me, just do what you're going to do.

BILL

I'm going to shower then. Are you gonna—

HILLARY

no, I'm gonna stay up, and—

BILL

okay.

HILLARY

. . .

(Bill exits.

Hillary alone.

Soft knock on the door. Hillary opens the door—it's Mark.

Mark enters.)

MARK

I wanted to come by and show you the plan for tomorrow, the schedule, the—because I've updated it, there are some new things on the schedule.
I added some events, some additional appearances

HILLARY

alright, thank you, Mark.

MARK

. . .

HILLARY

. . .

MARK

Bill's here, isn't he.

HILLARY

. . .

MARK

I just heard that he's here from some random person in the hallway—

Is Bill in there, in the—?

HILLARY

Yes.

He's taking a shower.

MARK

Why?

HILLARY

He needed a shower.

MARK

No, why is he here?

HILLARY

I called him, Mark.

MARK

You asked him to come here?

HILLARY

Yes.

MARK

But I asked you not to

HILLARY

it's really not any of your business

MARK

well yes, it is actually my business

HILLARY

he's my husband

MARK

that and a couple of other things too.

Can I ask why you brought him here?

HILLARY

I called him because I needed help

MARK

that's my job

HILLARY

what

MARK

helping you

HILLARY

helping me win?

MARK

yes

HILLARY

and I'm losing.

MARK

. . . What can I do.

HILLARY

Tell me the truth.

MARK

About what.

HILLARY

You've asked enough people enough questions to know what they really think of me—

Are people rooting for me? Or
do they just wanna see bad shit happen to me,
see me dragged through the mud—

MARK

of course not

HILLARY

are you telling me the truth
or do you not know the truth, or—
or do you know the truth
and you're just hiding it from me—

MARK

I would not do that

HILLARY

I'm not even sure that people see me as "human"

MARK

Is that something Bill said—?

HILLARY

I don't think Bill's the only one saying what Bill said.

MARK

You need to get Bill out of your head.

HILLARY

I need to know where I stand—
I need to know if anything I do
actually matters, or if it's like here I am over here
doing what I do, while what everyone out there
sees is something that has nothing to do with
me or what I'm actually trying to do—
This is a nightmare—it's like
I've got some kind of Hillary
twin, some kinda Hillary that

looks a lot like me, that everyone thinks
is me, but it isn't me, and it's out there doing
all sorts of things while
the real me is off asleep in bed—and then I get blamed
for it all when I wake up in the morning.

MARK

Alright.

Okay.

HILLARY

. . .

MARK

For starters:

HILLARY

. . .

MARK

—"being human"

is overrated.

"Being human"—what does that even mean?

You're human.
You have emotions.
You feel things.
You *might* show it differently from some people—
Doesn't mean those
feelings, those qualities aren't there.

What else did Bill say,
what other critiques did he have of our—

HILLARY

story

MARK

what about it

HILLARY

says I don't have one

MARK

of course you—

HILLARY

what is it?

MARK

I mean, *you're* Hillary.
You've been around.
People have known you for years.
You're familiar.

HILLARY

That's not really a story, is it.
It's more of a—I don't know—
it's not a—

MARK

not everything needs to be framed as a story—

HILLARY

still doesn't answer my question.

MARK

You're the mature, rational candidate—

HILLARY

(Unenthused) great—
You mean boring.

MARK

It *is* great.

You are boring.
Boring is good.
It says that what you're doing
isn't about you,
but about the "work"—everything that needs to get done
to make people's lives just a little bit better.

And that's the thing you have that Bill never had,
and the thing that Bill *did* have, he doesn't have that anymore.

He lost his touch.
People aren't interested in Bill like they used to be.
They're tired of him.
And putting him with you
will make them tired of you—
tired of you before they've even gotten any of you,
because that's the thing—they haven't—they haven't
actually gotten you yet.

You *are* new, in a way.
And and and we're
just waiting for the clouds to clear
and for people to see you
exactly the way you are,

and they will,
they
will.

You're Hillary.
Not Hillary Clinton.
Just
Hillary.
That's your story.

HILLARY

(Sober) . . . right.

MARK

. . .

HILLARY

. . .

MARK

—hey, why don't you just get some sleep and—

HILLARY

I have a story, Mark,
and it isn't what you say my story is.
No . . . My story is this:

I'm the woman who used her husband to get into politics.
I'm the woman whose husband screwed around.
And I'm the woman who let her husband screw around.
Why? Because I'm the woman who
wanted into politics so bad—
so bad that she would let her husband
screw around because she thought

that if she left her husband, she would have
no chance of advancing her career.

That's what people think.
Whether or not it's true—
and it's not true—still
that's what people think.

And I am trying to change my story, Mark.
But that's my story.
And any new story I give them
is just a less-interesting second act to the first.

MARK

. . .

HILLARY

Thanks, Mark—
this has been very illuminating.
You can leave now.

MARK

. . .

(Mark leaves. Hillary shuts the door behind him.

Silence—Hillary all by herself.

After a bit . . .

She takes out the coin.

She stares at it.

She flips it.

Looks at it . . .)

HILLARY

heads . . .

(Flips it again.)

. . . heads

(Flips it again.)

. . . heads?

(Flips it again.)

what the fuck?

(Flips it again.)

Tails.

. . .

Okay.

This will be good.
This is the right thing to do.
This is—

(To audience) End of Act One.

(Just a slight pause, a breath.)

Act Two.

(Enter Mark and Bill.)

Two days later,
Mark comes to my hotel room with the news
that I . . .
won—that I won?
—how the hell did I win—?
It's so weird that I won

MARK

we stayed on course,
we did everything we planned to do

HILLARY

but still, how did I go from here to here, how—

MARK

a lot of people are saying that they feel like you found your voice

HILLARY

my voice

MARK

yes

HILLARY

what does that even mean?

MARK

It means people are listening to you.

HILLARY

What changed that they're listening when they weren't before?

MARK

I think people were excited about Barack,
that there was excitement over the "new,"
over—a "new voice"—and so that got some attention
for a bit and—

HILLARY

I don't know

MARK

you don't—

HILLARY

no, I think—you know what it is—?

I know what it is.

Two nights ago
I was convinced,
fully convinced—you saw me—
you saw how I was—
that I was done.
That there was no way
that I could possibly win.
And I think knowing that—really *knowing* that—
I
just
gave
in.
I just said to myself, I'm gonna lose—? then I'm gonna lose.
That's it.

Stop trying.
Stop trying to win—
just get to Tuesday and take that loss.
And I got okay with it—with the idea of losing,
and I think somehow
by going out there and going out there to lose,
that made losing harder
and winning easier.

BILL

That's not why you won.

HILLARY

Oh it's not.

BILL

No.

HILLARY

Tell me why I won, Bill.

BILL

You won because you took my advice

HILLARY

oh—!

BILL

and the advice worked, it—

HILLARY

what are you talking about?

BILL

You know.

HILLARY

I don't.

BILL

What did I tell you about—

HILLARY

being a broken mess?

BILL

Yes.

HILLARY

How exactly is any of what I did in the past day any part of *that*?

BILL

. . . The luncheon.

HILLARY

The luncheon, what.

BILL

The luncheon with the women, the women's luncheon
that you were at yesterday

HILLARY

okay

BILL

you were talking—

HILLARY

yes

BILL

you were answering questions

HILLARY

I was

BILL

and they were asking you about family and balancing that with this—with running the country, and the difficulty of doing both and
you started to cry—

HILLARY

No, I didn't—!

BILL

you started to tear up

HILLARY

I did not go out there and
fake some tears in order to win a—

BILL

not saying you *faked* it—

HILLARY

Mark, did I "cry" at the luncheon—?

MARK

. . . I don't know.

BILL

You did.

MARK

It might have looked like you did.

HILLARY

Are people *saying* I cried?

MARK

. . . well yes but—

HILLARY

I remember the question
and answering the question, but I definitely don't remember crying—
are people saying that's why I won?

MARK

I think it's that they're saying you found your voice

BILL

and they're saying that because you cried.

HILLARY

I mean *maybe* my eyes got a little watery,
maybe it was allergies, maybe—
maybe I was tired
I *was* up until four A.M.—

BILL

Doesn't matter whether or not you really cried—
people think you cried,
and now they see you as a *real* person.

(A cell phone starts ringing.)

HILLARY

It's just that—I'm sorry—I just don't buy it—
Mark, get me a tape or something of this—I
have to see it for myself

MARK

okay.

(Mark answers his phone on his way out.)

Yeah?
Hold on—

(Mark leaves the room, door shuts.)

HILLARY

. . .

BILL

. . .

HILLARY

. . .

BILL

Come on. Admit it.
It feels good

HILLARY

what

BILL

winning

HILLARY

to you or to me?

BILL

Admit it.
Come on.
I see a smile—
You don't wanna show you're smiling, but you're—

HILLARY

yes, winning is something that does feel good—

BILL

Jesus—!

HILLARY

but—

BILL

like pulling teeth here

HILLARY

but I can't quite trust it—

because just one day ago I was losing,
and losing really bad,
and I don't want to get too happy and
have it thrown back in my face—
wake up tomorrow and find I've gone back to losing. I
can't stop wondering if there's a shoe that's gonna drop—

and there's also the money problem, that's—

BILL

no

HILLARY

well

BILL

I gave you the money.

HILLARY

What money.

BILL

What money—?
The money you were asking for—
I transferred some money from me to you.

HILLARY

. . .

BILL

. . .

HILLARY

. . .

BILL

Don't believe me?

HILLARY

. . . no, it's just very unexpected—

It's just very . . .

BILL

. . .

HILLARY

. . . well

thank you.

BILL

. . .

HILLARY

Thank you, Bill.

BILL

We're meant to do this together.

We're very good together.
We can be two different things—
I can be the dog, your attack dog—go out there
and attack your opponents—
and you can be the mother, the mommy, the nurturing, caring—
everyone wants a mommy and everyone wants a dog,
and with us they get both.

I couldn't have won without you back in '92,

but also, you can't win this without me, not now—

HILLARY

but I did.

BILL

No you didn't.

HILLARY

Again, because of the crying thing—?

BILL

No.

HILLARY

What do you mean "no"?

BILL

. . .

HILLARY

. . .

BILL

. . .

HILLARY

What do you mean—

(Mark reenters.)

no, Mark, not now

MARK

we need to talk

HILLARY

later

MARK

Bill, would you mind stepping out for a moment so Hillary and I can have a—

BILL

I would mind, Mark—

HILLARY

what is it, Mark

MARK

so Bill—
it turns out—

made one or two appearances
on your behalf.

HILLARY

. . .

BILL

. . .

MARK

Did you know about this—?

HILLARY

of course I didn't—did you—?

MARK

no

HILLARY

how did you not know—?

MARK

I—

BILL

didn't need to know—
you two needed to stay focused on the things
you were focused on

HILLARY

what exactly happened.

MARK

Bill went out to—

HILLARY

No, I don't want to hear it from you,
(To Bill) I want to hear it from you.

Bill.

Speak.

BILL

I went to your staff, I asked them if there
were maybe one or two places I could help out,
and they seemed really excited about the idea,
really thought it could be a lot of help.

HILLARY

What did you say when you showed up to these places?

BILL

What do you think I said? I said people
should vote for you,
I said you were the most qualified candidate,
I said you had the most experience, that—

HILLARY

(To Mark) Is that right?

MARK

Not exactly.

HILLARY

What exactly did you say?

BILL

I don't remember every single word—

HILLARY

Mark?

MARK

He attacked the press,
he claimed they were biased,
he claimed that they were going out of their way
to make you look bad,
and out of their way to make the other guy
look better—called them liars—

and

he spoke for a while about your opponent.

HILLARY

What did he say about my opponent.

MARK

He called Barack illegitimate.

HILLARY

Illegitimate.

MARK

Uh-huh.

HILLARY

What's that code for, Bill?

BILL

It's code for nothing—it's code for—

HILLARY

what do you think people think when
they hear you say that, when you say
"he's illegitimate"

BILL

it just means he's not legitimate—he's not a legitimate candidate. He doesn't have the experience you have.

HILLARY

I think people hear something else
when they hear you say that, and I think you know that,
which is why you said it.

BILL

People will think what they think—I can't be responsible for every—

HILLARY

oh for fuck's sake

BILL

do I have to make clear everything I'm not saying

HILLARY

in some cases—yes.
You do.

BILL

. . .

HILLARY

. . .

BILL

I don't know why you're looking at me like
I'm the bad guy here.
You won.

HILLARY

If I won because of what you went out there and said,
then it's credit to you. If I won because of
what I did yesterday,
then, again, it's credit to you because I
followed your winning advice.

BILL

No what I'm saying is we need each other.
That alone, we're not so good. We're lesser.
But, together—we're very successful

MARK

and you know where I stand on this—

BILL

Fire him.
Just fire him already— You wanna
talk about sabotage—

MARK

how exactly did I—?

BILL

You brought her the deal

MARK

what deal

BILL

running mate?
Remember that?
the offer that would have ended the campaign
before it even started

MARK

I didn't "bring" her that offer

HILLARY

he did not bring me any deal—he did not suggest—

BILL

then why was he telling you about it in the first place

HILLARY

to try to make me feel better

BILL

and did it?

MARK

It would have been wrong to keep it a secret.

BILL

That's bullshit. Your job—do you understand your job—?

MARK

I'm pretty sure I do.

BILL

I'm pretty sure you don't— Your job
is to tell her only what she needs to know—
needs to know to get to the next day—the next hour,

the next minute—because when you're in her position—
our position—doing the kind of thing we do—
that we're doing—
we can't know everything.
That's detrimental.
But you don't understand—you can't understand that
because you're just a pollster.
Where we—she and I—actually go out into the world,
put our faces in front of people,
put our names on the line,
and make decisions that matter.
You just ask a couple of questions and add up some numbers.
So how does that put you in any position
of knowing what we do or do not need to know?

MARK

I think I have perspective.

BILL

What gives you perspective?

MARK

Not being where you are,
not being the person who's running for office,
but being the person who's standing
next to the person who's running—

BILL

No, that just means you don't know what you're talking about.
Perspective is having been there.
Perspective is having experienced it.
Sure, it's easy to act like you know what you're
doing when you're not involved,
when you're sitting on the sidelines saying things like,

"Well that's not how I would've done it,"
but the point is you're not doing it.
You just sit there
and watch other people do
what you wish you could do,
while you yourself do nothing at all.
And that
that
is why no one will remember you
when you're dead.

MARK

. . .

BILL

. . .

MARK

Maybe no one will remember me when I'm dead,
but how will people remember *you* when you're dead.
What's the first thing that people will think when
they hear your name
years from now?
What do you think? What do you *really* think?
If you were gonna put money on it.

Will they remember you for the work you did for this country?
Will they remember—will they be able to say, "Oh, Bill Clinton,
yeah, he's that great president who did
this or that to trade policies.
Bill Clinton—who balanced the budget"—will they say that?

"Don't ask don't tell"?
You'd probably prefer people forget that.
But at least that's something presidential.

But you know—you know—that's not
what they'll remember you for.
They'll remember you for fucking around.
They'll remember you for the most stupid
embarrassing—simply reckless
set of circumstances.
that almost got you kicked out of the job and jeopardized—

(A phone rings.)

HILLARY

hold that thought.

(Hillary picks up.)

Hello?

oh

okay

yeah, no now's not the best time—

no

no

oh, I see—

uh-huh—

Okay.

Yeah, sure.

Okay.

Bye.

(Hillary hangs up.)

MARK

. . .

BILL

. . .

HILLARY

. . .

MARK

Who was that?

HILLARY

. . .

MARK

Who were you talking to?

HILLARY

Barack's people.

MARK

What did they want?

HILLARY

. . .

MARK

I imagine they were pretty upset about what Bill said about him

BILL

I imagine they know it's a primary and / people say what they need to say—

MARK

hey, on your campaigns we do things how you / like, and on Hillary's we do—

BILL

I imagine that she'd like to win, I imagine—

HILLARY

I took the deal.

I took the running mate deal.

MARK

. . .

HILLARY

And he's coming over here to talk about it,
I assume—

MARK

you—

HILLARY

Sunday night, I called him and said I wanted the deal.
And so I'd think he's coming over here
because he thinks it's a little strange that I told him I'd lose,
and then the next day my husband goes out and
starts campaigning for me,
and then I win.

BILL

. . .

HILLARY

. . .

MARK

Why did you take that deal?

BILL

(To Mark) Because of you.

HILLARY

(To Bill) No, this is because of you.

This is because you just seem to follow me around like a stench I can't shake.

And it's because I was losing—
because I knew winning wasn't possible,
and because I don't want to disappear.

So yeah, faced with the very strong likelihood that I was going to lose and lose bad,
I'd sooner take second place with the hope that
taking second now would
keep me around a little bit longer
so that maybe I can still have a chance
of taking first, later—
not now,
but also not never.

BILL

. . .

MARK

. . .

HILLARY

. . .

MARK

Alright. Well then
that's it for me.

HILLARY

What does that mean—?

MARK

there's nothing for me to do here

HILLARY

there's still a campaign

MARK

that you're trying to lose

HILLARY

isn't that what you were already doing to begin with.

MARK

. . .

HILLARY

I'm sorry for saying that—well not really—

MARK

No, I need to go.
I need to go because I'm scared that if I stay

and he stays
and we stay together,
then at some point I'm gonna punch him in the face,
I swear I'm just gonna punch him right in the face,
and he'll probably fall and have a heart attack,
and then I'll look really bad—he'll have really deserved it—
but I'll look really bad—like I was trying to
beat up and kill an old guy—
an old guy that everyone inexplicably likes.

And everyone will hate me for it,
and my life will be ruined.

And when I die, I *will* be remembered,
but only as the guy who punched Bill Clinton in the face.
And I don't want to be remembered for that.
I'd rather not be remembered at all
than be remembered for that.

So I'm going to go now,

and don't try to convince me to stay.

HILLARY

. . .

MARK

. . . right.

HILLARY

. . .

BILL

. . .

MARK

. . .

HILLARY

. . .

(Mark exits.

Just Hillary and Bill, alone.)

. . .

BILL

. . .

HILLARY

You happy?

BILL

You're making it really hard to be.

HILLARY

Excuse me?!?

You came out here—

BILL

because you called me

HILLARY

and you got yourself everything you wanted—right / down the list

BILL

and what is it that you think I wanted—?

HILLARY

Mark's gone, I cried, and you got to go out there
and be back in the spotlight—

BILL

all of which got you exactly what you wanted—so don't
try to act like—

HILLARY

Did you think I wasn't going to find out—?
huh—? that you'd gone out there and
started stumping after I asked you not to?

BILL

Sure, but I also figured you'd win, and when you'd
won, you wouldn't care, because you'd understand that
everything I did
I did to get you that win.

Little did I know you were *trying* to lose!

HILLARY

I don't think of it as losing,
I think of it as a different path—
a new start without you

BILL

Bull shit.
You only took that offer because you didn't want to lose.
You'd sooner tank your campaign yourself than
lose because you lost—because—

HILLARY

go—

BILL

you're not gonna give me this one, are you

HILLARY

go before he gets here.
I want to speak with him myself,
without you here,
without your getting in the middle—

BILL

so that I can't save you from making a terrible, irreversible mistake—?

HILLARY

because I don't trust you. Because
you did everything I asked you *not* to do,
because you don't listen, because
you've never listened—
Sure, you listen to other people—but not to me you don't—
No, I have to hear everybody go on about how
great it is to meet you,
how you're so amazing and inspiring,
always talking about how when they talk to you,
they always feel so heard,
so listened to—
that you make them feel as though
they're the only person in the world who
matters to you in that moment.

And that's great for them, but when do I get to experience that?
Huh?
When do I get this magnificent version of Bill
that everyone else seems to get except for me—? you know,
I'd like to meet that Bill,

I would—I would very much love
to spend some time with him and
to get the chance to feel the way all of those other people
get to feel.
But no.
The Bill I get doesn't notice I'm here,
the Bill I get tramples me time after time,
the Bill I get is a pretty shitty Bill.

And you know what—what really pisses me off:
is the thought that
you get
the best version of me,

while the version of me that everyone else gets
is drained and used up and stale and wooden—that's
what you called me—your words not mine—
Well do you ever think that maybe you might have some part
in me being so drained and stale and wooden?

And you come in here with your cute little sob story—your
hang-dog-woe-is-me-sad-sack performance—
trying to make me feel bad for you—how
"oh no" the—whatever he was looking at your stomach—
tells you you're cursed.

No, Bill, not you—
I'm cursed.
I'm the one cursed here,
and you
are the curse.

BILL

You have no idea what a curse is—

I hope you never experience a real curse—because a curse—a *real* curse
is being someone who did something,
did something wrong, and keeps apologizing for it,
but the apologies never take, and for however many times I apologize,
it's never enough.
It's never enough.

HILLARY

I forgave you, years ago

BILL

no, no no no no—no something changed.
Years ago—something changed
and it never changed back.

HILLARY

Okay. Alright.
You want to help, do you really—?

BILL

I do.

HILLARY

Then you can go out there
and tell everyone
how much
I helped you
during those eight years,
how much I've advised you—from the very beginning—
how pretty much anything that was
any good about your presidency
was because of me,

because of my ideas,
because of my guidance, because of—

Would you do that,
would you actually—

BILL

that's not a winning strategy, Hill,
that's not going to—

HILLARY

aw go fuck yourself, Bill—
you refuse to give credit where credit is due.

BILL

Is that what this is all about—please don't tell me that this is why you're running for the presidency just to get some kind of credit you think you're owed?

HILLARY

No, I'm not running to get credit—

I want to do this because I actually think—no, I *know*—
I'd be great at this job,

because for decades, I've been sitting over to the side, waiting,
watching—watching other people do
what I know I can do better.
Watching other people who don't know
what they're doing get ahead of me,
sitting here, having the better ideas first,
while other people stumble through and get it wrong
again and again until they get it right,
if they ever even get it right.

BILL

. . .

HILLARY

I mean, let's just take this down to the bone:
What I really think

is that you want me to lose.

BILL

no—

HILLARY

you don't want to see me get this job,
and see me do a better job than you did when you had the job.
You don't want to be eclipsed, because you know—
you know—that given the chance
I will eclipse you.

Mark's right, he's actually right—
Most people—that general public you're so fond of—

they actually can't name one thing that you did in office
that wasn't *that* "one thing."
And if you ask them what they liked about you,
what made you a good president—
all that's left, all that's remembered
is your personality.

That's it.

And if you ask me, that's some pretty thin stuff—
That's a pretty lousy thing to be remembered for.

BILL

. . .

HILLARY

. . .

BILL

There is no way that I am trying to stop you from
doing the thing you've always wanted to do.
I swear—I swear it to God—I swear—

I just want what's best for you.

HILLARY

What's best for me.

BILL

Yes.

HILLARY

I'll tell you what would be best for me, ya' know, because
Mark polled—he conducted polls—we have numbers
to tell us what
is and isn't best for me, and what's
actually best for me is for me to divorce you.

BILL

. . .

HILLARY

Divorcing you would be very good for me.
Divorcing you would completely change how people see me,
people would think more of me
if I ended it with you.

They'd have more respect for me—it's really what everyone wishes I had done way back when, and so when they look at me, what they see is disappointment.

And I did—I thought about it—
tried to imagine how it might feel to do something like that.

And I didn't do it.
Was I scared to do it—? oh God I don't know—
Did I actually *want* to stay married to you?
Did I think to myself well I've put so much time
into this relationship, it would seem wrong to let that go—
and I do have the memory of something—something that
feels very far from where we are now,
something that I miss and I
think you miss too.
But I also have to ask myself, what do I get from this
versus how much does it take away?

And I really don't want to stay in this marriage
if the reason I'm staying in it is for you,
is so that *you* don't feel bad,

You know—? enough "feelings."
Feelings make us do the stupidest things—
I want to stay in this marriage because I *want* to stay in it,
because I get more out of it than I lose—but Bill,
every second that passes I see myself losing more than I gain.

BILL

. . .

(There's a knock at the door.)

HILLARY

And there he is.

BILL

I don't know what to do.

HILLARY

Nor do I.

BILL

. . . You want me to go.

HILLARY

He's already here.

BILL

You wanna ask him to come back another time?

HILLARY

No.

BILL

Alright, well—

HILLARY

Let's just get this over with.

(Hillary opens the door.

Standing in the doorway is Barack. Instantly, she puts on a cheerier "public" face.)

Hello Barack

BARACK

Hi Hillary

HILLARY

how are you—

BARACK

good good—

HILLARY

come on in

BARACK

Thank you— Oh—! and Bill's here—

HILLARY

Bill / is here

BARACK

hey I did not know Bill would be here

HILLARY

have you two not met before—you / two introduce yourselves

BARACK

yeah I think we have / met, actually—

HILLARY

oh great great / great great—

BARACK

Hi Bill

BILL

good to see you.

BARACK

You too.

HILLARY

So!

BARACK

Well. Congratulations on the—

HILLARY

aw well thank you

BARACK

was really

HILLARY

unexpected.

BARACK

Yes.

Yes, it was.

HILLARY

Should we talk about that.

BARACK

Oh I don't know that there's anything that needs to be said about that

HILLARY

well, I would, I would like to talk about what's happened the past couple of days.

BARACK

. . . Alright.

HILLARY

I really did not expect what happened yesterday to happen.

BARACK

And when you refer to what happened yesterday, you're talking about—

HILLARY

the win

BARACK

sure

HILLARY

I didn't mean to

BARACK

because that's not what it looks like

HILLARY

I know

BARACK

from the outside looking in,
it looks like a—a concerted effort to win

HILLARY

I know

BARACK

there was a change in strategy,
some kind of revamping of your campaign—the staff—

the addition of Bill, and—I mean I even just heard—
just coming in here—just in the hallway there—that you let go of Mark—?

HILLARY

Yes and no

BARACK

you understand how it looks from my vantage point.

HILLARY

I do

BARACK

so

HILLARY

but when I took the deal—
That wasn't some kind of underhanded sneaky
way of trying to
screw you over—

BARACK

oh well—but even if it was

HILLARY

and it wasn't

BARACK

but hold on, hold on: If it was
I would understand.
It's not as if we had anything in writing—
there was no obligation to me. You did what you had to do,
and maybe, maybe I let my guard down—my mistake—

and you took advantage of the situation, of me, of—
You could call it a betrayal,
but one person's betrayal is another person's
reasonable action—you
have to do what you have to do—
So, I get it—it's not what I would have done,
but it's legitimate.

HILLARY

Mistakes were made—hey you'll make mistakes too.

BARACK

Clearly, I already have.

I'm trying to avoid making more.

HILLARY

. . .

BILL

. . . Can I explain what happened—?

HILLARY

No, Bill. I'll explain—
(To Barack) I'm gonna ask that you keep all of this . . .

BARACK

alright.

HILLARY

The reason I had to fire Mark is because Mark called up Bill
and sent him out on the trail. Without my approval.
Now I was very clear with Mark that I intended to bow out
and take you up on your offer,

that I'd become your running mate,
but of course that would mean that Mark would be out of a job,
and, as you can imagine, he couldn't really
get on board with that idea,
so he got Bill involved.

BILL

And, if I may

HILLARY

go ahead

BILL

when I got the call, I had no idea about the running mate deal.
If I had known about that—had known what Hillary wanted—
I would have never come to New Hampshire.
But I just assumed because Mark was calling me that
he had Hillary's approval—

HILLARY

it was Mark who told Bill to be aggressive,
told him to go on the attack

BILL

and I really should have known better,
because I knew—
I *know*—that that's not what Hillary would have wanted—
that has never been her strategy—
I *should* have asked her myself, but I didn't
and I went out there and said all sorts of things
that I'm ashamed I said.

HILLARY

So that's why I had to let Mark go.

BILL

I'm going back home—
tomorrow morning, I'm leaving—
I'm leaving this campaign to Hillary—
it's up to her what she wants to do,
if she wants to bow out and be your running mate,
that's her choice

BARACK

well that offer is off the table.

Now you do understand that right—?
I thought you understood—the running mate deal—

HILLARY

I wasn't asking for it.

BARACK

Right

HILLARY

no I want you to be *my* running mate.

BARACK

Wait, what?

BILL

. . .

HILLARY

Same offer you offered me—?

BARACK

so you're . . .

HILLARY

offering it back to you.

BARACK

I don't think that's something I would even—

HILLARY

don't answer "no" yet, don't—

BARACK

I'm not interested

HILLARY

but you will be.
You will be interested in it, when I'm done explaining to you
why you should be interested in it—
And I'm only making this offer just this once,
so, when you walk back out that door, that's it,
your chance has passed.

BARACK

. . .

HILLARY

I think you're going to do well.
I do—next couple of primaries—
you'll win some more states.
But then I'm going to win some more,
and then I'll go on to win more than you win

BARACK

you know this

HILLARY

I do

BARACK

how

HILLARY

because you're a blank slate.

BARACK

A what?

HILLARY

The reason you're doing as well as you are right now,
is because you're a blank slate—there's nothing on you.
you're telling people just enough, but not enough,
so that they can fill in the blanks of what you're saying
with all the thoughts that make them happy,
that make them feel good—but you've not told
them enough for them to know
where and how they disagree with you.
You're just hovering in this safe spot.
And it's working.
For now.
But there's gonna come a point where you *do* say a little more,
and when you do—they're going to see all the ways
in which there's a distance, all the ways
in which they disagree with you, all the ways
you come up short of where they want you to be.

And when that happens it's going to feel like a big betrayal.
And there's gonna be a drop-off—a big drop-off—
and you'll lose a lot of support.

But unlike you: with me there's nothing left to discover,
and so there's not going to be a drop-off.
I'm just going to stay steady where I am.

Now because you'll have been doing well up until that drop-off,
when you lose, you'll lose slowly.
Your loss will be a long drawn-out loss.
And the problem is:
people don't forget long losses.
Long losses stain, they linger—
And so when you do lose with a long drawn-out loss,
you don't get a second chance.

But—

if you drop out—you can be my running mate.
We'll win.
And then after me,
you'll get your turn to be president,

plus you'll have the experience—experience—
let's be honest—that you don't have right now—

You go in there now—sure you have ideas—you have energy—but it will take you four years to learn how to do any of it, and by then it will be too late. The people who want to end you will have formed their attack, and you'll be on the defense for the next four if you get a next four.
Look at what happened to him.
(Pointing at Bill) Isn't that right, Bill?

BILL

. . . Pretty much.

HILLARY

Do you want what happened to him to happen to you?
Because that right there is your future if you don't
make the right choice right now.

BARACK

. . .

HILLARY

So—

What do you think?

BARACK

. . . uhhhhhh

. . . What do I think.

HILLARY

. . .

BARACK

Well I think
we're at a crossroads here.

I think the decisions we make in this room,
moving forward,
are really important—
really really important.

And I think
we need to consider our options

very carefully.

HILLARY

I'm not sure what you mean by that.

BARACK

So back about a week ago
when I told the people who work with me—I told them
my idea, that you and I would run together, they
didn't like the idea because, honestly, they didn't like you—
they didn't trust you, but
I said "no,"
I said, "make the offer, I want to make the offer,"
and they did, even though they were against it.

I really didn't think you would say yes,
but then you did,
and I was really happy that you did,
but the people who work with me weren't, and
the moment you said yes,
they started digging.
They started digging and looking for a reason
why you and I should not work together.

(Barack produces an envelope.)

This is
actually
why I'm here.

I wanted you to see this.

(He hands it to Hillary.)

HILLARY

What is it?

BARACK

Nothing good.

HILLARY

(Opening the envelope) What—something about Bill?

BARACK

It does pertain to Bill.

HILLARY

Something about the old scandals, the old—
the stuff that people have been talking about for—?

BARACK

That's not what it's about. Just—
read it.

(Hillary reads.)

HILLARY

. . .

BILL

. . .

HILLARY

. . .

BILL

What is it?

BARACK

Sorry, Bill. This is really awkward. I didn't realize you'd be here.

BILL

Can I see it?

BARACK

. . . So basically, the gist of it, Bill, is that
you've been receiving a lot of money
in connection with this charity work,
you get paid to go around and get in front of people
and talk up the work of some good people
trying to do some good things, and
you benefit and they benefit, and—
seems like everyone benefits.
But where the money comes from—the money that
funds the people who give *you* the money—
where *that* money comes from is where the problem is—
because there's a pretty direct line from
one to the other that makes it look like you're profiting
from, frankly, some of the very worst people in the world—

BILL

but it's just not true— This is all taken way out of context—

BARACK

what context is the right context?

BILL

Just about any money—if you look at it from the wrong angle—
can look bad

BARACK

I really don't think you *meant* to do anything wrong

BILL

it's not that I didn't mean to—
it's that I didn't do anything wrong.

BARACK

But it looks like you did, see,
and if it looks like you did, then it doesn't matter
whether you did or didn't.
This looks bad, it is bad.

BILL

But even if it looks bad,
it looks bad for me, not for her.
This has nothing to do with her.

BARACK

But has her campaign—has your campaign
received money from Bill?

HILLARY

. . .

BARACK

. . .

HILLARY

. . .

BARACK

. . .

BILL

. . .

BARACK

so, you see.

HILLARY

It looks bad—so what.
You know it's all so much more complicated than that,
but now you go and put this out there, that just makes you—

BARACK

I'm not releasing this.

HILLARY

Okay, well good

BARACK

but someone will.

It's just a matter of time.

HILLARY

Then we'll just have to do something about that.

BARACK

I actually think there's only one thing you can do,
if you're serious—

HILLARY

what

BARACK

leave the race

HILLARY

no, I don't think so—

BARACK

bow out and take this thing with you,
so that it doesn't blow up and cause a lot of collateral damage,
for all of us.

HILLARY

. . .

BARACK

And maybe . . . maybe if you bow out now,
bow out before all this comes out,
maybe it won't ever come out and—
maybe it'll just
go away and never become anything.

And maybe what this is is it's just bad timing.
Maybe it's not your time,
and maybe it's my time—I tend to think it is—
I have a really good feeling it is—and
maybe I'm wrong,
but if it is my time,
that doesn't mean you won't ever get your time,
Your time just might not be now,
but later.

HILLARY

Don't tell me when my time is or isn't—

I have not put in years of hard work and sacrifice—
of getting knocked around and humiliated—
just to let a little piece of paper
make me pack up and go home.

I'm sure—I have no doubt—that there are
more little pieces of paper
where this came from—about God knows what—
I'll deal with those like I'm gonna deal with this one,
and I'll keep moving forward—I refuse
to let all problems become my problem.

That's not right.
That's not fair.

My feeling is just as strong as your feeling—
and I think it's my time.

BARACK

. . . Alright, well, just think about it, will you—?

HILLARY

and you—you think about it too—
think about my offer to you.

BARACK

Okay . . .

I'm gonna leave you two.

It's good to see you, Bill.
Good to see you, Hillary.

Sorry to have to—you know—

HILLARY

oh no, no, I really appreciate the heads-up.
We're gonna work on figuring this out, fixing this
little—I don't even want to call it a
problem—I'm really not worried about—

BARACK

alright.

(Barack exits.)

HILLARY

. . .

BILL

. . .

HILLARY

. . .

BILL

. . .

HILLARY

. . .

BILL

. . .

HILLARY

. . .

BILL

. . .

HILLARY

. . .

BILL

What are you thinking.

HILLARY

. . .

BILL

. . .

HILLARY

. . .

BILL

What are you thinking.

HILLARY

. . .

BILL

. . .

HILLARY

. . .

BILL

Alright . . .

HILLARY

. . .

BILL

here's what I think . . .

HILLARY

. . .

BILL

I think
you should
divorce me.

HILLARY

. . .

BILL

If you stay married to me,
you're tied to me, and
you're tied to all the mistakes I've made

But if you divorce me—
you said it yourself—people will see you
in a new light. They'll have a respect for you that
they never had before.

And I'll go my way and you can go yours,
and I'll do what I do, and
if I make more mistakes, it won't matter,
or it won't matter as much as it would matter now,
and what I do won't hurt you as much as it hurts you now.

I think it's what would be best.
I think it's the only way.

HILLARY

Do you want that?

BILL

Does it matter?

HILLARY

I wish it didn't, but . . .

BILL

. . . No.

I don't want that.

HILLARY

You're sure?

BILL

Oh, yes.

HILLARY

Why.

BILL

Because you're all I have.

You are— You're all I have.
But if I have you,
you're left with nothing.

HILLARY

. . .

BILL

. . .

HILLARY

(To audience) I look at Bill.
He looks at me.
Neither one of us knows what to do.
I turn on the TV for the first time in days.
And there it is—they're playing the clip of me at the luncheon,
the luncheon with the women,
and I watch the TV and I see myself.
And I see myself doing what looks like crying.

It really looks like I'm crying.

But I don't remember it,
but I also know that it doesn't matter
what I remember or what I think I did.

All that matters is what it looks like,
and it looks like I was crying,
and so maybe that means that that's what's true—I just don't know anymore.

And then I turn off the TV.

(The room gradually goes dark. A field of stars begins to appear, and the entire hotel room seems to disappear right in front of our eyes.)

We walk out on the balcony.
We look up at the night sky.
We see stars.

And the stars that I look at are the stars that
everyone has looked at.
Everyone great and small.
Important and unimportant.

I say to Bill . . .

One hundred,
two hundred,
maybe even three hundred years from now,
your name will be a name that people will know
like they know the stars above . . .

but I'm down here,
and it's like I'm trying to stare at the back of my own head,
trying to see something that I just can't see,
but if I could catch a glimpse of it,
then I would know what to do.

It's all off,
in a subtle but deadly way
everything is off.

And Bill tells me

BILL

I know how you feel

HILLARY

and I know that he does,
but also not really.

And while I'm staring at the stars,
I think about the universe,
and how—if the universe is infinite—and some people say that it is—that means there are an infinite number of
planet Earths exactly like ours,
And there are universes in which Bill is president,
but there are also universes in which I'm president,
and there are universes in which I'm president and Bill is not,
and there are universes in which neither of us is president
and where everyone else is president except for us.
If the universe is infinite all possibilities exist . . .

but I am starting to realize . . .

I'm starting to realize that I live
in one of the universes where I don't win.
And this is hard. It is hard to think that he got it and I can't—

and I'm fighting to win.
I'm fighting to win and I know I can win,

but I can't win.

(The stars extinguish.)

END OF PLAY

LUCAS HNATH's plays include *A Simulacrum*, *Dana H.*, *The Thin Place*, *Hillary and Clinton*, *A Doll's House, Part 2*, *Red Speedo*, *The Christians*, *A Public Reading of an Unproduced Screenplay about the Death of Walt Disney*, *Isaac's Eye*, and *Death Tax*. He has been produced on Broadway at the John Golden and Lyceum Theatres; Off-Broadway at The Atlantic, Playwrights Horizons, New York Theatre Workshop, The Vineyard, Soho Rep., and Ensemble Studio Theatre; and premiered work regionally at the Goodman, Center Theatre Group, Humana Festival of New American Plays, Victory Gardens, and South Coast Repertory. He is a New York Theatre Workshop Usual Suspect, a member of Ensemble Studio Theatre, and an alumnus of New Dramatists. Awards: Whiting Award, Guggenheim Fellowship, Kesselring Prize, Outer Critics Circle Award for Best New Play, Obie Award for Playwriting, Steinberg Playwright Award, Windham-Campbell Literary Prize, Lucille Lortel Award, and a Tony Nomination for Best Play.